MA 8/14

ELIZABETH I

Damian Harvey

Illustrated by Rupert Van Wyk

W
FRANKLIN WATTS
LONDON • SYDNEY

Contents

CHAPTER 1
It's a Girl

Elizabeth Tudor was born in Greenwich, England, on the 7th September 1533. Her father, King Henry VIII, wasn't happy.

Her mother, Anne Boleyn, was worried. She loved her baby girl but she knew that her husband wanted a son.

King Henry needed a male heir
to inherit the throne when he
died. He grew impatient waiting
for his wife to give him a son.

Soon, he started spending more
time with her lady-in-waiting,
Jane Seymour.

Then, before Elizabeth was even three years old, King Henry announced that her mother was guilty of treason.

Anne Boleyn was arrested and taken to the Tower of London to be executed.

Elizabeth never saw her mother again.

A few days later, King Henry married Jane Seymour, his third wife.

The following year, on the 12th October, they had a son. The King was delighted.

Elizabeth hardly saw her father until she was nine years old. She often felt lonely but the King's sixth wife, Catherine Parr, looked after her.

The Princess enjoyed spending time with her older stepsister, Mary, and their little stepbrother, Edward, at Hatfield House, near London.

Elizabeth spent a lot of time studying.

She learned Latin, French and Spanish and proved herself to be very clever indeed.

When King Henry died, his son, Edward became King of England. He was only nine years old.

Edward wasn't King for long. He became ill and died when he was just fifteen years old.

CHAPTER 2
Bloody Mary

It was soon decided that Elizabeth's stepsister, Mary Tudor, should become queen as she was the eldest. Many people didn't like Queen Mary.

Queen Mary was strongly Catholic like her mother, Catherine of Aragon. She thought everyone else in England should be Catholic too.

Queen Mary punished people who refused to follow the Catholic religion. Some were executed.

This made Queen Mary even more unpopular. Some people called her 'Bloody Mary' because she could be very cruel.

13

Elizabeth was a Protestant like her father, Henry VIII. He had fallen out with the Catholic Church after the Pope refused to let him divorce Catherine of Aragon, his first wife.

Lots of people looked to Elizabeth as their only hope and thought she would be a much fairer queen than her stepsister.

Some of the people rebelled against Queen Mary and there was a lot of fighting. Mary's advisors were worried that Elizabeth might be plotting against her too.

When she was only 19 years old,
Elizabeth was arrested and locked in
the Tower of London.

It was cold and damp in the Tower.
Elizabeth was frightened that she
was going to be executed just like
her mother had been.

Then, after a few months, Elizabeth was released from her prison. As she was taken away from the Tower, people cheered in the streets.

It was clear that Elizabeth was becoming even more popular.

But she still wasn't free. The young princess was taken to a large house and kept under guard.

When Elizabeth was 25 years old, Mary became ill and died. Elizabeth was declared Queen of England.

CHAPTER 3
Queen at Last

Elizabeth was crowned in
Westminster Abbey on the 15th
January 1559. Crowds of people
lined the streets and cheered as she
went by in her carriage.

Elizabeth was determined to make
England a better place to live, but
it wasn't going to be an easy job.
The country was sharply divided
between Catholics and Protestants.

She carefully chose advisors and ministers to help her rule the country. But it was Elizabeth who had the final word and this didn't always make her advisors happy.

Elizabeth was tired of the fighting between Catholics and Protestants.

She wanted Britain to be a peaceful place. She strengthened the ties with the Church of England. People could choose their own religion in private so Catholics and Protestants would both be happy.

There were lots of other problems
that needed sorting out, too. The
towns and cities were crowded with
people looking for work and they
were becoming dirty, unhealthy
places to live.

Lots of people begged for money
on the streets. Beggars were treated
harshly. Elizabeth passed a new Poor
Law that meant people had to pay
money to help the poor.

Elizabeth had lots of friends but never got married. Her ministers thought this would cause problems.

Elizabeth didn't have any children so they worried about who would rule the country after she died.

They worried even more when Elizabeth caught smallpox.

Elizabeth was determined to rule
by herself and keep the peace.

She also knew that no matter
who she married it would upset
someone and cause more trouble.

"I don't need a husband," she
declared. "I am married to my
kingdom."

CHAPTER 4
Sink the Armada!

Elizabeth enjoyed meeting brave sailors like Francis Drake and Walter Raleigh.

She loved hearing about their adventures as they travelled around the world in search of gold, jewels and rare spices.

They sound like pirates.

How exciting!

They told her about the Spanish ships they had sunk and how they brought tobacco, potatoes and treasure to Britain.

During his adventures, Francis Drake became the first Englishman to sail all the way around the world on his ship, the *Golden Hind*.

Spain was a powerful Catholic country. King Philip II of Spain was angry with Queen Elizabeth. He didn't like Sir Francis Drake sinking his ships, and he wasn't happy about all the Protestants in England.

Like many other Catholics,

Philip thought that Elizabeth's cousin Mary, Queen of Scots, should rule England. People plotted to kill Elizabeth and put Mary on the throne. Mary was taken to prison. Elizabeth wouldn't believe her cousin was to blame.

Mary stayed in prison for 19 years. Elizabeth's advisors eventually convinced her that Mary was guilty of treason and she was executed.

King Philip of Spain was furious and
made plans to invade Britain. He
started to build a huge fleet of ships,
known as the Spanish Armada.

Elizabeth heard about this and sent Francis Drake to investigate.

When he arrived in Cadiz in Spain, Francis sank lots of Spanish ships and brought back a huge cargo of treasure.

After this, it took King Philip
longer than planned to get his
Armada ready.

Finally, in 1588, the Armada was
spotted sailing along the coast.
There were over 120 ships filled with
soldiers ready to invade England.

King Philip II was determined to
teach the English a lesson.

But the English were ready for them.

Queen Elizabeth impressed the
people of England by visiting her
troops at Tilbury Docks before the
battle began.

Led by Francis Drake, the English Navy faced the Armada as it sailed up the Channel. They managed to split up the Spanish Armada and the scattered ships were shipwrecked during terrible storms.

No English ships were lost at all. It was a huge victory for the English Navy and a huge victory for Queen Elizabeth, too.

CHAPTER 5
Changing Times

Elizabethan England was prospering.

At the new theatres being built
in London, people watched plays
written by William Shakespeare and
Christopher Marlowe.

Elizabeth didn't have to go to the theatre like everyone else. She watched plays in the Royal Court.

Although Elizabeth was getting older, she still wore fine clothes and bright red wigs.

When Elizabeth caught a cold,
everyone thought she would get
better, but she knew she was going
to die and refused to go to bed.

Elizabeth had to decide who would
rule the country after she died. She
chose King James VI of Scotland, the
son of Mary Queen of Scots.

Elizabeth gave a final speech to the people of England. They called it her 'Golden Speech' and her words were remembered long after her death.

"And though you have had, and may have, many mightier and wiser princes sitting in this seat, yet you never had, nor shall have, any that will love you better."

Elizabeth was queen for 45 years, longer than many kings and queens before her.

She helped bring about peace between England and France and also between the Catholics and Protestants in England.

She won the hearts of the people with her great speeches and determination. Even now she is remembered as Good Queen Bess.

You can go and visit her tomb in Westminster Abbey where she was buried next to her sister, Mary.

Timeline

1533   Elizabeth Tudor is born.

1536   Elizabeth's mother, Anne Boleyn, is executed at the Tower of London.

1547   Elizabeth's father, Henry VIII, dies. Her brother Edward becomes King Edward VI.

1553   King Edward dies and Mary Tudor, Elizabeth's sister, becomes Queen.

1554   Elizabeth is imprisoned in the Tower of London by Mary I. She is released two months later.

1558   Queen Mary dies and Elizabeth is crowned Queen.

1559   Elizabeth's coronation takes place in Westminster Abbey.

1562   Elizabeth I is ill with smallpox.

1587   8th February: Mary, Queen of Scots is executed.

2nd April: Sir Francis Drake sails to Cadiz, Spain and destroys the Spanish ships, bringing back their cargo.

1588   The Spanish Armada reaches the English coast. It is defeated by the British Navy.

1601   The Poor Law changed. Now it stated that parents and children should care for each other.

1603   Queen Elizabeth I dies at the age of 69.

First published in 2014 by
Franklin Watts
338 Euston Road
London NW1 3BH

Franklin Watts Australia
Level 17/207 Kent Street
Sydney NSW 2000

HB ISBN 978 1 4451 3301 0
PB ISBN 978 14451 3302 7
Library ebook ISBN 978 1 4451 3304 1
ebook ISBN 978 1 4451 3303 4

Dewey Decimal Classification Number: 942'.055'092

Series editor: Melanie Palmer
Series designer Cathryn Gilbert

Printed in Great Britain

Franklin Watts is a division of Hachette Children's Books,
an Hachette UK company.
www.hachette.co.uk